RAINTREE BIOGRAPHIES

Frederick Douglass

Pat Lantier

RAINTREE
STECK-VAUGHN
PUBLISHERS

A Harcourt Company

Austin   New York
www.raintreesteckvaughn.com

Published by Raintree Steck-Vaughn Publishers, an imprint of Steck-Vaughn Company.

Project Editors: Sean Dolan, Leigh Ann Cobb, Sarah Jameson
Production Manager: Richard Johnson
Designed by Ian Winton

Planned and produced by Discovery Books

Library of Congress Cataloging-in-Publication Data
available upon request.

ISBN 0-7398-5674-X

Printed and bound in China
1 2 3 4 5 6 7 8 9 0 07 06 05 04 03 02

Acknowledgments
The publishers would like to thank the following for permission to reproduce their pictures:
Cover & p.4 Corbis; p.5 Mary Evans Picture Library; pp.6 & 7 Peter Newark's American Pictures; pp.8, 9 & 10 Bridgeman
Art Library; p.11 Corbis; p.12 Peter Newark's American Pictures; p.13 Bridgeman Art Library; p.14 National Park Service,
Frederick Douglass National Historic Site; pp.15, 16 & 17 Peter Newark's American Pictures; p.18 National Portrait Gallery,
Smithsonian Institution; p.19 Bridgeman Art Library; p.20 Corbis; p.21 National Park Service, Frederick Douglass National
Historic Site; pp.23 & 24 Corbis; p.25 Peter Newark's American Pictures; pp.26 & 27 Corbis; p.28 Allan Harris; p.29 Corbis.

CONTENTS

A PASSION FOR LEARNING

From his hiding place behind the heavy wooden door, the boy listened closely to the argument in the next room. His master, Hugh Auld, was scolding his wife for teaching the young slave how to read. Mrs. Sophia Auld was a kind woman who treated Frederick with affection. She had seen no harm in teaching the boy the letters of the alphabet. Master Auld, however, put an end to this instruction. He was very angry with his wife. He told her it was illegal to teach a slave how to read, and that it was also morally wrong. A slave with an education would eventually want his freedom.

"*Though conscious of the difficulty of learning without a teacher, I set out with high hope, and a fixed purpose, at whatever the cost of trouble, to learn how to read.*"
Frederick Douglass, in his *Narrative of the Life of Frederick Douglass.*

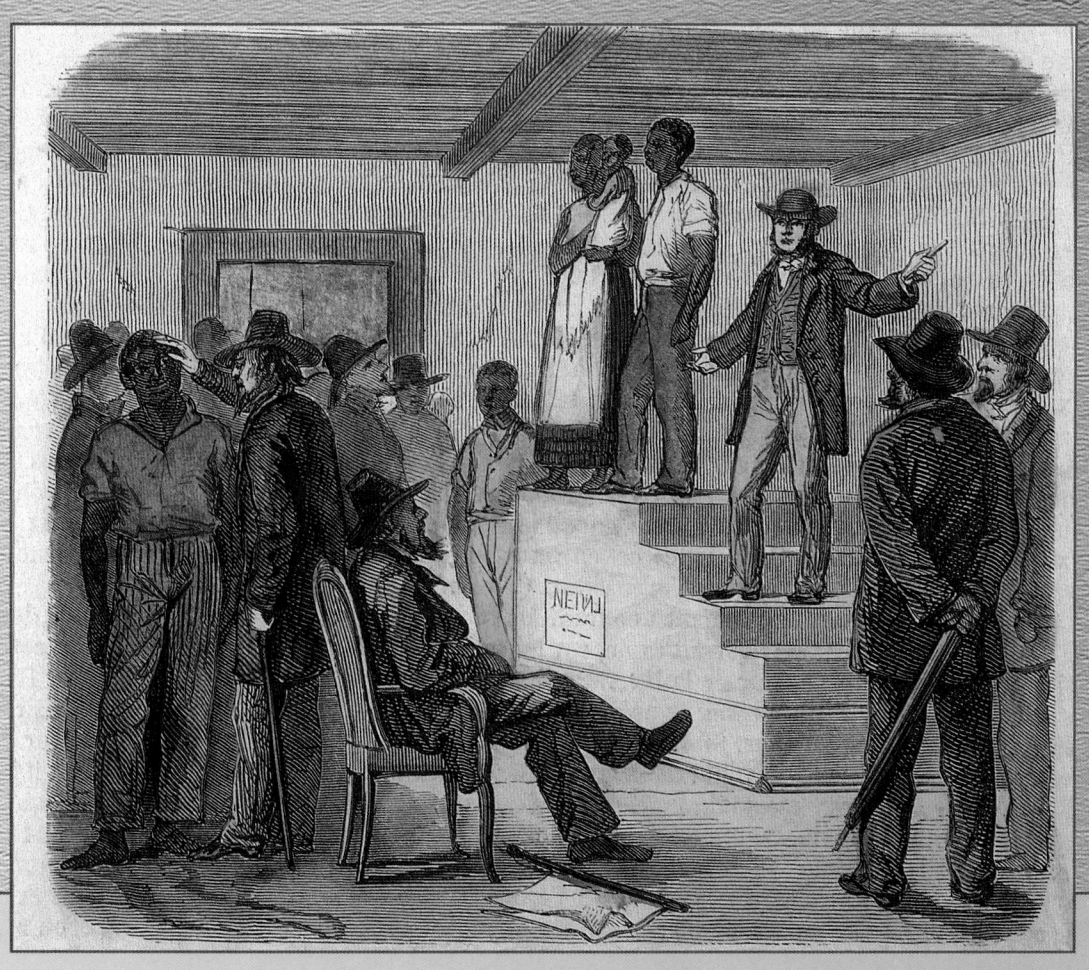

THE SLAVE ECONOMY

By the mid-18th century, there were four million slaves in the U.S. providing cheap and readily available labor for agriculture as well as mining and railroad construction. Slaves were put on public display and sold at auctions, most often in large towns and cities. Families were frequently broken up and sold off to different masters.

Frederick heard the argument in despair. Mrs. Auld's kindness and instruction had given him hope for a better future. Even though he was still young, the boy knew that learning to read and write was very important. It was the key to one day escaping the bonds of slavery. He would not give up his education. He would simply find another way to learn.

EARLY CHILDHOOD

Frederick Augustus Washington Bailey was born a slave in 1818 on a large wheat plantation in eastern Maryland. Frederick's mother, Harriet Bailey, was also a slave on the plantation, which included many small farms as well as a main house. He did not know his father.

For the first six years of his life, Frederick lived with his grandparents in a small house on the outskirts of the plantation. Betsey and Isaac Bailey took care of all the slave babies until they were old enough to work. It was not uncommon, though, for slave children to be cared for by relatives.

Many field slaves worked from dawn until dusk, with only the most basic amounts of food and water to keep them going. Overseers often used whips to make them work faster.

Huge cotton plantations like this one in the Deep South required many slaves to work the land. A special machine called the cotton gin was invented in 1793, which helped make cotton a very profitable crop.

Frederick saw his mother only a few times, and always at night. After working hard in the fields all day, Harriet had to walk 12 miles (19 km) to her parents' house to visit her son and then be back at work before sunrise the next day. The young boy remembered his mother as being beautiful and having a soft, loving voice. Harriet died when Frederick was still very young.

When Frederick was 7 years old, his grandmother took him to the main plantation house. He did not want her to leave him, but there was no choice. This was the real beginning of his life as a slave.

LIFE IN BALTIMORE

Frederick was always cold and hungry at the main house. Like the other slaves, he slept on a damp dirt floor with only a thin blanket to keep him warm. He had one long shirt to wear, and it had to last an entire year before he could get a new one.

When Frederick was sent to live in Baltimore, pictured here, he quickly learned the advantages of city life. A city slave usually had more privileges and freedom of movement than a plantation field slave.

In 1826, when he was 8 years old, Frederick was sent to Baltimore to live with the family of his master's brother, Hugh Auld. Mrs. Sophia Auld made sure Frederick had enough food and warm clothing, and treated him with respect.

When Mr. Auld ordered his wife to stop teaching Frederick to read, he was determined to learn some other way. While out running errands in the streets of Baltimore, he began trading pieces of bread with poor white children in return for short lessons in reading and spelling.

SLAVE AND MASTER

Masters had complete control over their slaves from birth to death. A child born to a slave mother was a slave, even if the father was a free man. Some owners hired out their slaves to do work elsewhere, on neighboring plantations or in the city, but they were rarely allowed to keep the money they earned. Posters, like this one from 1829, advertised forthcoming slave auctions.

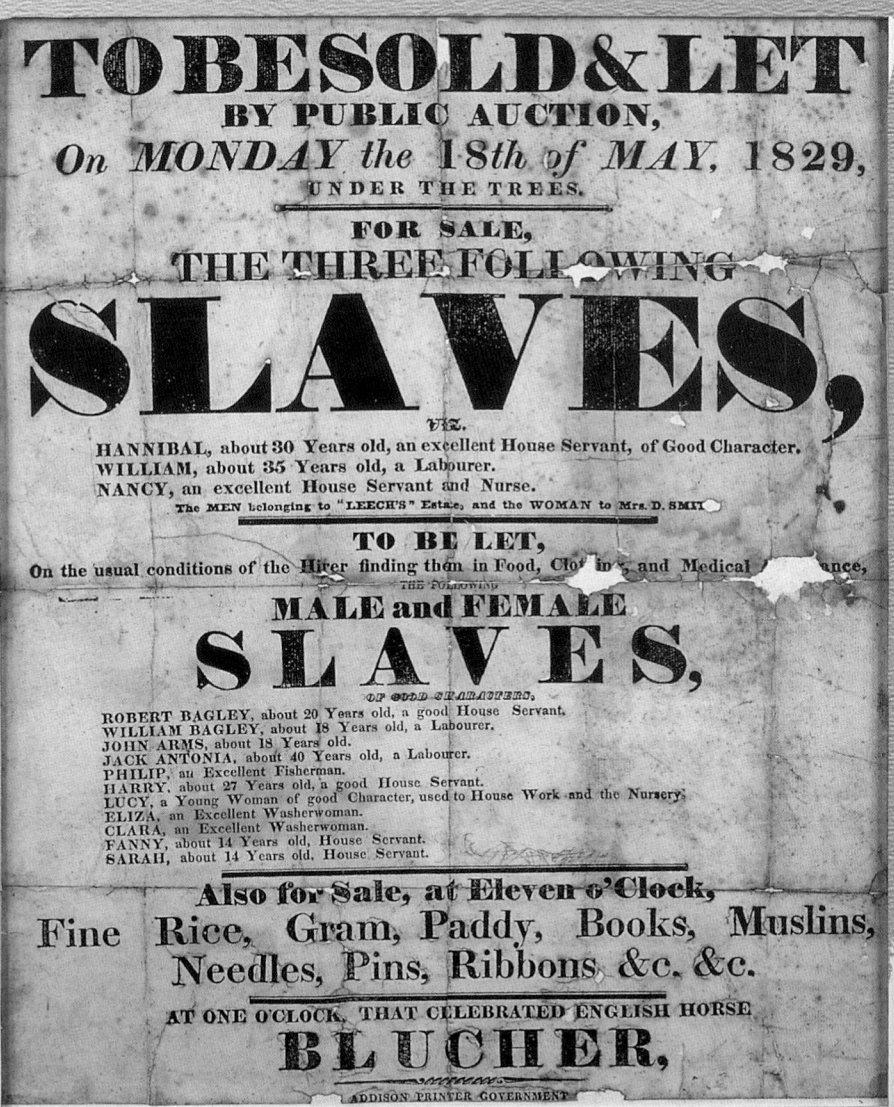

TO BE SOLD & LET
BY PUBLIC AUCTION,
On MONDAY the 18th of MAY, 1829,
UNDER THE TREES.
FOR SALE,
THE THREE FOLLOWING
SLAVES,
VIZ.
HANNIBAL, about 30 Years old, an excellent House Servant, of Good Character.
WILLIAM, about 35 Years old, a Labourer.
NANCY, an excellent House Servant and Nurse.
The MEN belonging to "LEECH'S" Estate, and the WOMAN to Mrs. D. SMIT
TO BE LET,
On the usual conditions of the Hirer finding them in Food, Clothing and Medical Assistance,
THE FOLLOWING
MALE and FEMALE
SLAVES,
OF GOOD CHARACTERS.
ROBERT BAGLEY, about 20 Years old, a good House Servant.
WILLIAM BAGLEY, about 18 Years old, a Labourer.
JOHN ARMS, about 18 Years old.
JACK ANTONIA, about 40 Years old, a Labourer.
PHILIP, an Excellent Fisherman.
HARRY, about 27 Years old, a good House Servant.
LUCY, a Young Woman of good Character, used to House Work and the Nursery.
ELIZA, an Excellent Washerwoman.
CLARA, an Excellent Washerwoman.
FANNY, about 14 Years old, House Servant.
SARAH, about 14 Years old, House Servant.
Also for Sale, at Eleven o'Clock,
Fine Rice, Gram, Paddy, Books, Muslins, Needles, Pins, Ribbons &c. &c.
AT ONE O'CLOCK, THAT CELEBRATED ENGLISH HORSE
BLUCHER,
ADDISON PRINTER GOVERNMENT

BACK TO THE LAND

In 1833, when he was 15 years old, Frederick was called back to the plantation in Maryland. Captain Thomas Auld was a cruel master who was never satisfied with Frederick's behavior. He wanted to crush Frederick's strong spirit, so he sent the boy to Edward Covey, a man known for "breaking" young slaves.

The working conditions of slaves were not improved by the invention of the cotton gin. Huge numbers of slaves spent back-breaking days in the hot sun, planting, hoeing, tending, and picking the profitable cotton crops.

For one year, Frederick toiled in Mr. Covey's fields. Because he was not used to this sort of labor, he was not very good at it and was beaten at least once a week. After months of cruel treatment, Frederick was exhausted and starving, and he began to lose hope.

One day, Frederick refused to let Mr. Covey beat him. He decided to resist, to fight back if necessary. They struggled together for more than two hours. Although Edward Covey would never admit that he had failed to "break" Frederick, he never tried to beat the young slave again.

It was during this time that Frederick decided he would not live his entire life as a slave.

"O that I were free!…Only think of it; one hundred miles straight north, and I am free!…It cannot be that I shall live and die a slave….There is a better day coming."

Frederick Douglass, in his *Narrative of the Life of Frederick Douglass*, **1845**

Frederick Douglass wrote about his experiences as a slave in his autobiography, Narrative of the Life of Frederick Douglass: An American Slave, *published in 1845. It was a very successful book.*

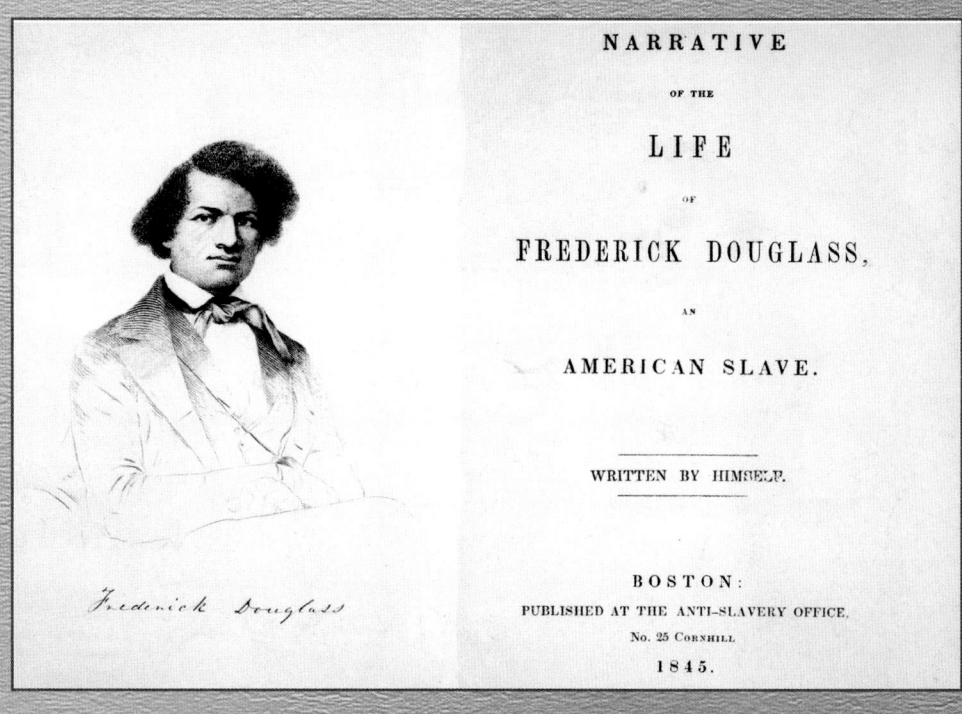

A First Attempt at Escape

When his year with Edward Covey was over, Frederick was hired out to William Freeland. Frederick still had to work in the fields, but Mr. Freeland was not a cruel man.

Frederick made friends on the Freeland farm, and he also made plans with some of them to run away. Five slaves planned their escape in secret, and Frederick forged permission papers for everyone involved so they could make their way more easily to freedom. On the day of their escape, however, their plan was discovered. The slaves were arrested and put in jail. Although the men eventually were returned to their original masters, Thomas Auld decided to send Frederick back to his brother in Baltimore.

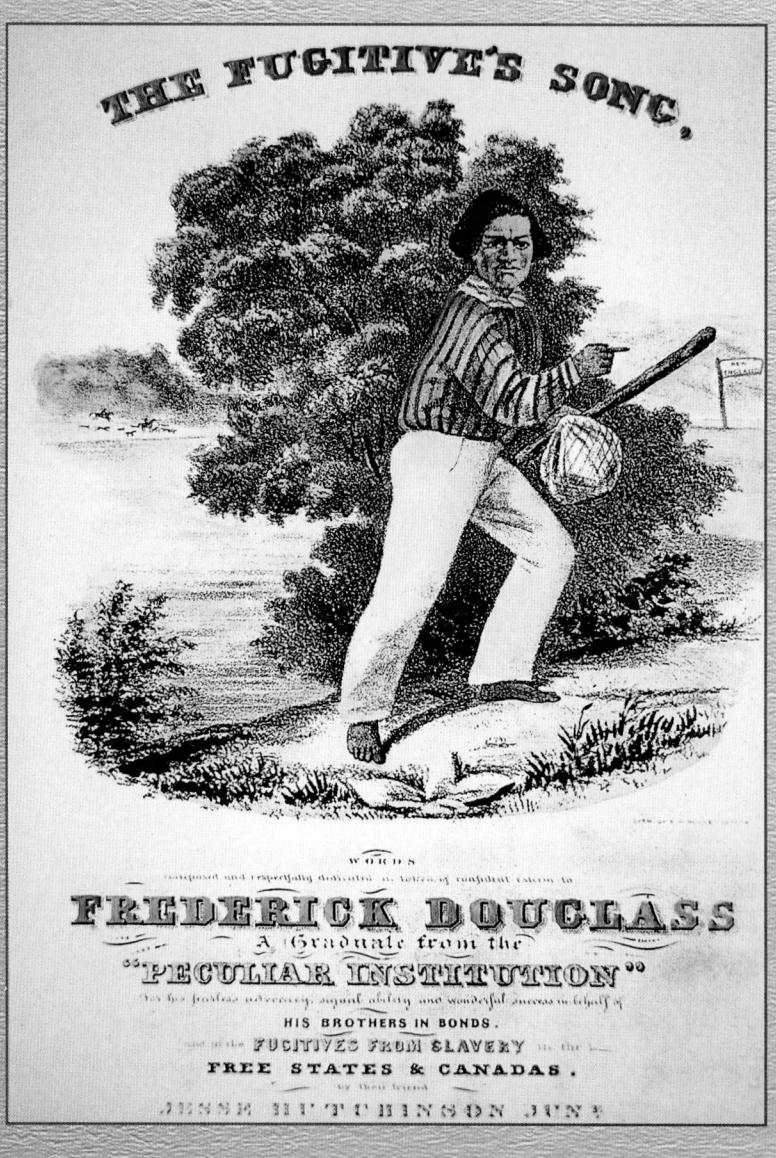

The Fugitive's Song *was composed in 1845 to honor Douglass, who had courageously escaped to freedom from slavery. This is the cover of the sheet music for the song.*

In the 1830s, the city of Baltimore was one of the country's busiest ports. It had a thriving shipbuilding business on the eastern side of the harbor.

Hugh Auld helped Frederick find a job as a caulker in the Baltimore shipyards. Each week, after many long hours of work, his wages were sent directly to Thomas Auld. Frederick was not allowed to keep any earnings for himself and became more determined than ever to escape.

"The slave is a human being divested of all rights, reduced to the level of a brute. He can own nothing, possess nothing, acquire nothing but what must belong to another."

Frederick Douglass, in an article in the *North Star*, Dec. 5, 1850

ESCAPE TO FREEDOM

Frederick had some spare time because of his employment as a tradesman. He set out to educate himself and soon began to attend meetings of free black people who gathered once a week for lectures, concerts, and readings. At these meetings Frederick learned more about the anti-slavery movement in the North, and gained great skills as a public speaker. Here he met Anna Murray, a free woman who worked as a servant for a wealthy Baltimore family. They fell in love.

Anna Murray was a source of strength and courage for Frederick. It was through her financial efforts that he was able to escape from Baltimore to New York, where he immediately made arrangements for her to join him.

Frederick became even more discontented with his status as a slave. In 1838, after an argument with his master, Frederick borrowed a friend's sailor uniform and protection papers and escaped from Baltimore by train. He arrived in New York two days later, on free soil, but not officially a freed slave. At first he did not know what to do, since he did not know anyone and had no money or place to stay. After a few days, he found the home of David Ruggles, a "conductor" on the Underground Railroad, who kept him safe until plans could be made for his future.

THE UNDERGROUND RAILROAD

The Liberty Line, or Underground Railroad, was a network of people that provided safety for runaway slaves. Although their work was against the law, they helped transport thousands of slaves from the South into free northern and Canadian territory.

THE LIBERATOR AND ABOLITION

Anna Murray joined Frederick in New York, and they were married. Mr. Ruggles advised Frederick to change his name to protect himself from being captured as a runaway slave, so he changed his last name to Douglass.

Frederick and Anna moved to New Bedford, Massachusetts, where Douglass found work as a laborer in the shipyards. Although Massachusetts did not approve of slavery, racism was common and made life difficult. Wages were low, yet Douglass was happy because he could keep the money he earned.

The first edition of The Liberator *appeared on January 1, 1831. Successful and influential in the fight against slavery, it remained in print for 35 years. This photograph shows an edition of the paper from 1859.*

William Lloyd Garrison (1805-1879), a passionate and dedicated voice in the fight against slavery, believed in a nonviolent approach. He aimed to educate others to the evils of the slavery system through his writings. He was also president of the American Anti-Slavery Society from 1843 to 1865.

Douglass was introduced to *The Liberator* and became passionate about this abolitionist newspaper, published by William Lloyd Garrison. Garrison believed all slaves should be freed and granted full citizenship in the United States.

> *"We rise in rebellion against a despotism incomparably more dreadful than that which induced the colonists to take up arms against the mother country; not on account of a three-penny tax on tea, but because fetters of living iron are fastened on the limbs of millions of our countrymen, and our most sacred rights are trampled in the dust....NO UNION WITH SLAVEHOLDERS."*
>
> **William Lloyd Garrison, *The Liberator*, May 31, 1844**

FIERY SPEAKER

Douglass proved to be a powerful speaker for the anti-slavery movement. When William Lloyd Garrison met Douglass in 1841, he immediately recognized this potential. He asked Douglass to become a spokesperson for the Massachusetts Anti-Slavery Society. Not only a strong debater, Douglass would share gripping recollections of his own life in slavery, making the issue even more real to his audiences. While he gave speeches in the North, Anna stayed home to care for their growing family.

"As a speaker, he has few equals." So wrote the editor of the Herald of Freedom newspaper about Frederick Douglass. This photograph of Douglass was taken in the 1840s, when he was in his 20s.

THE

ANTI-SLAVERY RECORD.

VOL. I.   MAY, 1835.   NO. 5.

CRUELTIES OF SLAVERY.

When we narrate the cruelties of individual masters upon their slaves, it is not for the purpose of exciting public indignation against those masters, nor of drawing the inference, that all masters are equally cruel; but to show that cruelty is the fruit of the system. Every tree must be known by its fruits. Cruelty may occur under good and impartial laws, but then it is in spite of the laws, not in consequence of them. On the other hand, where the laws themselves violate rights, make one class the property of another, and withhold redress of wrongs, cruelty, in ten thousand forms, is the necessary result. If the amount of cruelty perpetrated upon the slaves of this republic could be known to the world,

Vol. I.   5

People were impressed by Douglass's speeches. Some did not believe he was ever a slave because he was educated and spoke with such elegance. In 1845, Douglass published the first of his three autobiographies, *The Narrative of the Life of Frederick Douglass: An American Slave.*

THE ABOLITIONISTS

The Abolitionist Movement in the U.S. fought for the end of slavery and equal rights for all people. Abolitionists organized the Underground Railroad, and through their actions slavery became a national issue.

The book put Douglass at great risk since he was a runaway slave, and laws still protected the rights of the slave owners. When he heard Thomas Auld was trying to recapture his "property" and bring him back to Maryland, Douglass went to England.

THE NORTH STAR

Douglass toured England and the rest of Europe for two years, giving speeches and raising money for the anti-slavery movement in America.

When Frederick Douglass visited London in 1846, he was invited to speak to several groups about the issue of slavery in America. Douglass was well treated by everyone in England.

"What to the American slave is your Fourth of July? I answer, a day that reveals to him…the gross injustice and cruelty to which he is the constant victim….To him your celebration is a sham…a thin veil to cover up more crimes which would disgrace a nation of savages."

Frederick Douglass, in a speech given in Rochester, New York, on Independence Day, 1852

In 1846, two English friends raised enough money to buy Douglass's freedom from Hugh Auld. He was, at last, truly free. Douglass returned home in 1847 and moved his family to Rochester, New York. With some of the money he had earned in Europe, he started his own anti-slavery newspaper, the *North Star*, named after the star that guided slaves as they escaped in the dark of night to freedom. Many people said the paper would fail because Douglass was black and because he had no formal education. However, Douglass was sure about his abilities. This was his way of reaching more and more people and convincing them that slavery was wrong.

Douglass began publishing the North Star *in 1847. It was a large, single sheet published once a week, with an average circulation of 3,000 subscribers. It sold for 80¢ a copy.*

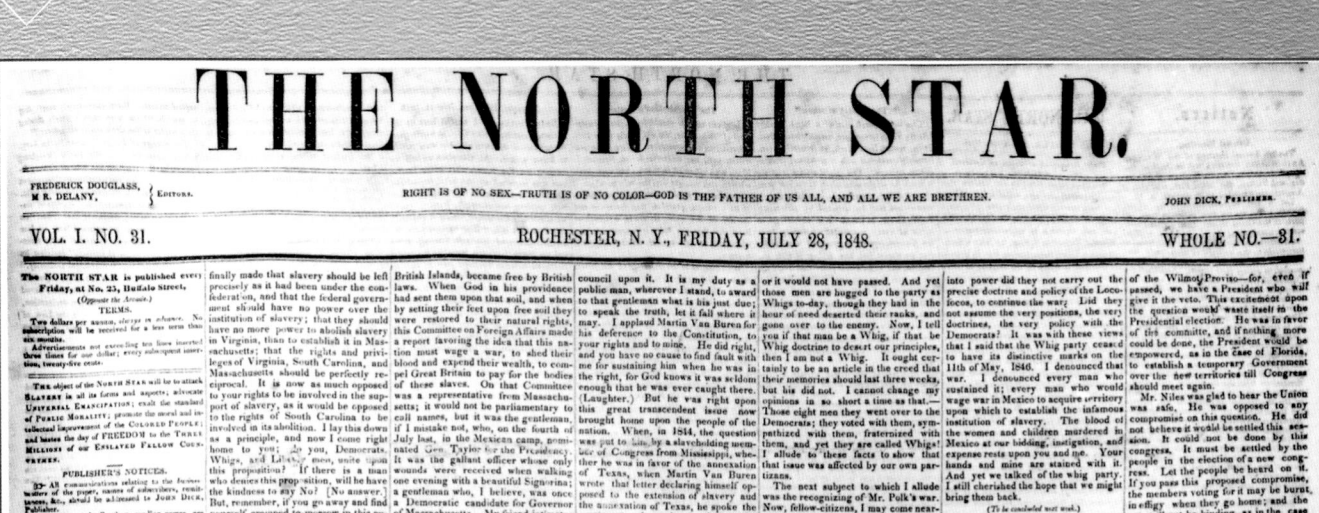

A COUNTRY DIVIDED

The United States was growing rapidly in the 1850s. Each territory that applied for statehood had to decide whether to be a slave state or a free state. The issue of slavery was tearing the country apart. In 1852, Harriet Beecher Stowe wrote *Uncle Tom's Cabin*, a book that quickly became famous as an argument against slavery. Mrs. Stowe admired Douglass and invited him to meet with her. They spoke about ways to educate former slaves so they could have a better life.

135,000 SETS, 270,000 VOLUMES SOLD.

UNCLE TOM'S CABIN

FOR SALE HERE.

AN EDITION FOR THE MILLION, COMPLETE IN 1 Vol., PRICE 37 1-2 CENTS.
" " IN GERMAN, IN 1 Vol., PRICE 50 CENTS.
" " IN 2 Vols., CLOTH, 6 PLATES, PRICE $1.50.
SUPERB ILLUSTRATED EDITION, IN 1 Vol., WITH 153 ENGRAVINGS,
PRICES FROM $2.50 TO $5.00.

The Greatest Book of the Age.

Written by a white woman from the North, *Uncle Tom's Cabin* reached a huge audience. Half a million copies had been sold by 1857. Abraham Lincoln later joked that this book helped cause the Civil War.

Douglass also knew John Brown, a fierce abolitionist who believed slaves should rise up against their masters. Douglass did not agree but respected his friend's position. In 1859, John Brown led a raid on Harper's Ferry, a military arsenal in Virginia. His plan was to give weapons to the slaves, who would then help him fight to gain their freedom. Brown held the arsenal for only a short time; he surrendered and was hung in December 1859.

Many people thought Douglass had helped John Brown plan the raid and should be arrested. Douglass went to England for a few months until his innocence could be proven. While he was away, his youngest daughter, Annie, died. Heartbroken, Douglass returned to his family in Rochester.

CIVIL WAR

The country was moving closer to war over the issue of slavery. Several southern states left the Union in order to protect their way of life. In 1861, Abraham Lincoln was inaugurated president of the United States. Soon afterward, the Civil War began.

Douglass proposed that black soldiers be allowed to serve their country. He helped recruit and organize two regiments of black Union soldiers, and two of his own sons enlisted to fight.

Black soldiers of the Massachusetts 54th Regiment charge the enemy at Fort Wagner, South Carolina, in 1863. The regiment became famous after this courageous assault demonstrated the heroism of black soldiers.

In 1863, Douglass convinced Lincoln and Congress to provide equal pay to black soldiers and to honor their achievements and bravery. That same year the Emancipation Proclamation went into effect, freeing the slaves in the Confederate states.

AFRICAN-AMERICAN SOLDIERS

More than 180,000 African Americans joined the Union army. They came from both southern and northern states. They fought in almost every battle of the long, bloody war, and more than 68,000 died battling for freedom.

The Civil War ended on April 9, 1865. The country was once again united, slavery no longer existed, and Lincoln was elected to a second term. On the night of April 14, 1865, however, President Lincoln was assassinated. The United States had lost a brave champion.

ELDER STATESMAN

Frederick Douglass had spent many years fighting for the freedom of his people. After the Civil War, his new task was to help black people gain equal rights as citizens of the United States. Many government officials looked to Douglass for advice and leadership, and he was offered a series of official posts by succeeding presidents.

In 1877, President Rutherford B. Hayes appointed Douglass, 60, U.S. Marshal for the District of Columbia. In this position, Douglass acted as overseer of the judiciary system in the nation's capital.

In 1877, Douglass purchased Cedar Hill, a nine-acre estate in Washington, D.C., and moved his family there. Five years later, Anna Murray Douglass died. Douglass missed his wife, who had always supported his efforts and taken great care in raising their children. Two years later, he married Helen Pitts, his former secretary. Many people objected to this marriage because Helen was white, but Douglass ignored the objections.

Douglass spent the last 18 years of his life at Cedar Hill. This stately Victorian home sits on a hill across the river from Washington, D.C. He continued to work from his desk in the library here until his death in 1895.

Douglass retired from public office in 1891, but he continued to work as a U.S. Marshal for the District of Columbia. He did not give up his struggle for the equality of all citizens of the United States. In 1895, Frederick Douglass died of a heart attack at Cedar Hill.

"Although it has at times been dark and stormy, my life in many ways has been remarkably full of sunshine and joy."

Frederick Douglass, in his *Life and Times of Frederick Douglass*, 1881

LEGACY

The remarkable life of Frederick Douglass provides a powerful example for young people today who want to achieve something valuable in their lives. Even as a young boy, Douglass bravely refused to accept a life of brutal bondage. He committed himself not only to escaping slavery and achieving personal freedom but also to improving the lives of others. He knew that the abolition of slavery was only the first step. What followed the Civil War was a different kind of battle—for equality and justice on all levels of American life.

A statue of Douglass, in honor of his contributions to the city and the country, was erected in Rochester, New York, in 1899.

A VISIT TO MR. AULD

In 1877, Douglass paid a visit to his one-time master, Thomas Auld, who was by then 80 years old. Auld admitted that he had never liked the system of slavery, and Douglass replied that they had both been victims of it.

The voice and spirit of Frederick Douglass—slave, caulker, freeman, husband, father, orator, writer, abolitionist, reformer, citizen, civil rights activist, and advisor to presidents—is still strong today, inspiring all who struggle to make the world a better place.

"To those who have suffered in slavery I can say, I, too, have suffered....To those who have battled for liberty, brotherhood, and citizenship I can say, I, too, have battled. And to those who have lived to enjoy the fruits of victory I can say, I, too, live and rejoice."

Frederick Douglass, in his *Life and Times of Frederick Douglass,* **1881**

J. Hoover's 1881 lithograph, Heroes of the Colored Race, *depicts Frederick Douglass (center) between two black U.S. senators, Blanch Kelso Bruce (left) and Hiram Rhodes Revels (right).*

TIME LINE

1818 Frederick Augustus Washington Bailey is born a slave on a plantation in Maryland.

1826 Frederick is sent to live with the Hugh Auld family in Baltimore.

1833 Frederick returns to work for Thomas Auld on the family plantation.

1834 Frederick is sent to work with Edward Covey, a slave-breaker.

1835 Frederick is hired out to William Freeland to work as a field hand.

1836 Frederick makes plans to escape but is discovered. He is sent back to Baltimore to live with Hugh Auld; works in shipyard as caulker.

1837 Frederick meets his future wife, Anna Murray.

1838 Frederick escapes from slavery and goes to New York. In this year, he also marries Anna Murray, changes his last name to Douglass, moves to Bedford, MA, and subscribes to William Lloyd Garrison's newspaper *The Liberator*.

1839 Daughter Rosetta is born.

1840 Son Lewis Henry is born.

1841 Douglass makes his first anti-slavery speech in Nantucket, MA.; William Lloyd Garrison hires Douglass as a lecturer for the Massachusetts Anti-Slavery Society.

1842 Son Frederick, Jr., is born.

1844 Son Charles is born.

1845 Douglass's first autobiography, *Narrative of the Life of Frederick Douglass: An American Slave*, is published. Douglass goes to Europe to avoid being arrested as a runaway slave.

1846 Ellen Richardson and Anna Richardson buy Douglass's freedom from Thomas Auld.

1847 Douglass returns from Europe; starts an anti-slavery newspaper, the *North Star*, in Rochester NY.

1849 Daughter Annie is born.

1855 Second autobiography, *My Bondage and My Freedom*, is published.

1859 John Brown's raid at Harper's Ferry; Douglass, a friend of John Brown, goes to England until it can be proven that he had nothing to do with the raid.

1860 Daughter Annie dies; Douglass returns home from England.

1860 Abraham Lincoln is elected 16th president of the United States.

1861 Civil War begins.

1863 Douglass helps recruit and organize two regiments of black Union soldiers.

1863 Lincoln signs the Emancipation Proclamation; Douglass meets with President Lincoln to protest the unequal treatment of black soldiers.

1865 Civil War ends; President Lincoln is assassinated.

1877 Douglass is appointed U.S. Marshall for the District of Columbia by President Rutherford B. Hayes; Douglass also purchases Cedar Hill.

1881 Douglass is appointed Recorder of Deeds for the District of Columbia by President James A. Garfield.

1881 Third autobiography, *Life and Times of Frederick Douglass*, is published.

1882 Anna Murray Douglass dies.

1884 Douglass marries former secretary Helen Pitts.

1889 Douglass is appointed Minister Resident and Consul General to Haiti by President Benjamin Harrison; serves until 1891.

1895 Douglass dies at Cedar Hill of a heart attack.

GLOSSARY

Abolish (uh-BOL-ish) To end, destroy, or do away with

Abolitionist (ab-uh-LISH-uh-nist) A person who works to end slavery

Arsenal (AR-suh-nuhl) A building or place where military weapons are manufactured and stored

Assassinate (uh-SASS-uh-nate) To kill or murder suddenly or without warning

Autobiography (aw-toh-bye-OG-ruh-fee) The life story or biography of a person told by himself or herself

Break (BRAYK) (verb) In the case of slaves, to destroy or crush the spirit of a human being, so that he or she will no longer fight the loss of freedom

Caulker (KAWK-ur) A worker who fills and tightens seams, joints, and windows in a ship or other structures so that water cannot leak

Conductor (kuhn-DUHK-tur) In the case of the Underground Railroad, a person who helps guide runaway slaves to freedom

Emancipation (i-MAN-si-pay-shuhn) The act of setting free. The Emancipation Proclamation of 1863 freed slaves in the United States from bondage

Inaugurate (in-aw-gyuh-RAY-shuhn) Through a special ceremony, to officially place someone in political office

Orator (OR-ate-ur) A person who has great skill in public speaking

Plantation (plan-TAY-shuhn) A large farm or estate used for growing crops and needing many laborers to do the work

Protection papers (pruh-TEKT-shuhn PAY-purs) Documents certifying status as a free seaman

Racism (RAY-sis-uhm) The belief or prejudice that members of one race are superior (or inferior) to another

Recruit (ri-KROOT) To gather or enlist people for military service

Regiment (REJ-uh-muhnt) A military unit that consists of a number of soldiers

FURTHER READING AND INFORMATION

Books to Read

Adler, David A. *A Picture Book of Frederick Douglass (Picture Book Biographies)*. New York: Holiday House, 1993.

McLoone, Margo. *Frederick Douglass: A Photo-Illustrated Biography (Read and Discover Photo-Illustrated Biographies)*. Minnetonka, MN: Bridgestone Books, 1997.

Miller, William. *Frederick Douglass: The Last Days of Slavery*. New York: Lee & Low Books Inc., 1995.

Schaefer, Lola M. *Frederick Douglass (First Biographies)*. Minnetonka, MN: Pebble Books, 2002.

Weidt, Maryann N. *Voice of Freedom: A Story About Frederick Douglass (Creative Minds Biography)*. Minneapolis, MN: Lerner Publications, 2001.

Woods, Andrew. *Young Frederick Douglass: Freedom Fighter (First-Start Biographies)*. Mahwah, NJ: Troll Communications, 1996.

Videos

Biography—Frederick Douglass. A&E Entertainment, 1997.

Frederick Douglass. Schlessinger Media, 1992.

Frederick Douglass: An American Life. Inner Visions Group, 1998.

Frederick Douglass: When the Lion Wrote History. PBS Home Video, 1994.

INDEX